642

THINGS TO WRITE ABOUT ME

BY THE SAN FRANCISCO WRITERS' GROTTO

INTRODUCTION BY JASON ROBERTS

CHRONICLE BOOKS

SAN FRANCISCO

CONTRIBUTORS

JD Beltran
Jenny Bitner
E.M. Boyd
Chris Colin
Lindsey Crittenden
Laura Fraser
Meron Hadero
Yukari Iwatani Kane
Diana Kapp
Ben Marks
Jennifer Mattson
Hunter Oatman-Stanford
Jason Roberts
Ethel Rohan
Ethan Watters

ISBN: 978-1-4521-4730-7

Manufactured in China.

Designed by Eloise Leigh
Typesetting by Kristoffer Branco

10 9 8 7 6 5 4 3 2 1

Chronicle Books LLC
680 Second Street
San Francisco, CA 94107

www.chroniclebooks.com

Chronicle books and gifts are available at special
quantity discounts to corporations, professional
associations, literacy programs, and other organizations.
For details and discount information, please contact our
premiums department at corporatesales@chroniclebooks.com
or at 1-800-759-0190.

Hello. We're the San Francisco Writers' Grotto, a community of more than one hundred professional writers working in just about every genre. Fiction, memoirs, nonfiction, short stories, journalism, poetry, screenplays, playwriting, new media productions, you name it—if it uses words to tell a story, we've written it. For more than two decades now, we've sweated over deadlines, celebrated triumphs, and commiserated over failures, then cajoled each other to get back to work and do it all over again. We've collectively written a very tall stack of books, movies, television shows, and print articles. In the process, we've garnered an equally impressive stack of rejection slips.

But enough about us. Let's talk about you.

642 Things to Write About Me, the latest in our bestselling series of kick-starters for the creative process, is the first to focus exclusively on the subject you're supremely qualified to discuss: yourself. This journal is a compendium of topics, crafted and curated to draw out aspects of your life well worth the telling. Families and friends, youthful hopes and fears, lost causes and lost loves—they're yours to remember, recount, and nurture into rewarding narrative detail. "The unexamined life is not worth living," Socrates famously declared. Consider this your exam.

These pages contain 642 acts of provocation. Engage with them randomly, methodically, or in the order they catch your mind's eye and spark introspection. We hope they'll illuminate a few surprising corners of your spirit and give rise to tales only you can tell.

JASON ROBERTS
San Francisco Writers' Grotto

Write a letter to the teacher (or coach) who made a difference in your life, asking him or her for help. What are you asking for? Why?

The dish your mom always cooked that you wished she wouldn't.
What did it look like, smell like, taste like?

_____

_____

_____

_____

_____

_____

_____

_____

_____

Picture a photo from your childhood, one you know well. Narrate the
scene around the taking of that photo, to the best of your memory.

_____

_____

_____

_____

_____

_____

_____

_____

_____

_____

What's the biggest position of power you've ever held?
How did it change you?

Write about the natural disaster experience you had, never had,
and/or wish you'd had.

What year was your year of maximum coolness?

Using the following template as a jumping-off point, write about a lesson you learned or an insight you gained. At the time, I felt/thought/acted _____. Now I see/understand/admit that_____.

What's the thing no one believes you can
actually remember?

What's the biggest leap of faith
you've taken?

The first time you realized that adults
weren't always totally truthful

You can choose any previous dream to dream
again tonight. Which one do you pick, and why?

Describe an accident you've been in. Were you at fault? Who was?
What excuses were made? What were the lasting consequences?

Write about your voice. Do you think it suits you? Would you change
it if you could? How has it changed over the years?

Write about the imaginary friend you had, never had, or wish you'd had.

What piece of jewelry do you wear most often? Write about why it's
your go-to-piece of jewelry. Where did you get it? What do you
like about the way it looks on you? Why does it feel good to wear?

Write about a good-bye that you didn't know was a last good-bye.

Write about the morning you least wanted to get out of bed.

Who was the hardest person in your life to forgive?
How did you do it?

Finish this sentence and keep writing for 10 minutes. DO NOT LOOK AHEAD.
What I most want you to know about me is. . . .
Stop. Now write this and keep going for 10 minutes: That was all a lie.
Here's what I really want you to know:

Your high school reunion is coming up. Think of one person you really don't want to see there. Write a letter to that person about what happened back in high school, and how it makes you feel, even today, this many years later.

Your family pet starts talking to you. What exactly does he or she think is going on around here?

You knew they were lying. You chose to pretend you believed them.

What's one way you might become eccentric in your old age?
How might you go in another (but equally batty) direction?

How did the way your parents felt about their bodies or physicality affect you and how you feel about your body and physicality?

What was your favorite trip as a child, and why?

What is the object that belonged to your parent that you associate most strongly with him or her, and why?

What's the most confused you've ever been? Tell that story.

That time you tried to do a job well, even though it was stupid

Write everything interesting you can about your worst scar (literal or figurative).

Write about your first vivid memory. Then write about all the ways
you might be misremembering or mistaking it.

Tell a family story that you think will be passed down and told generations from now.

Think of someone you know well. Write about what you'll never understand
about that person.

Have you ever owned an item but completely forgotten why you purchased it?
Write a fictional—but elaborately plausible—reason.

Write a one-page synopsis of your life. It's for someone who's in a hurry and not particularly interested.

Have you ever rekindled a friendship or personal relationship?
Why and how?

_____

_____

_____

_____

_____

_____

The time you went to bat for someone, and wished you hadn't.

_____

_____

_____

_____

_____

_____

Do you remember the first time you felt you had won an argument with a parent?
Does that still feel like a victory today?

_____

_____

_____

_____

_____

_____

Make a list of things you've probably done for the last time.
Say your good-byes.

_____

_____

_____

_____

_____

_____

_____

_____

What's the largest block of time you've ever had to kill?
How did you go about it?

_____

_____

_____

_____

_____

_____

_____

_____

_____

_____

Recount the day you put your favorite poster up on your bedroom wall.
Then write about the day you took it down.

Describe the supernatural experience you had (or never had but wish you did).

Think of a time you stood up for a stranger. Write a 10-line story about what happened and why you intervened.

Describe the first time someone relied on you, and how you felt.

Describe a place you've been to that's least like your hometown and explain why.

That relationship that ended: when did it really end?

Your worst enemy writes his/her memoir. There's a whole chapter devoted to you. How does it begin?

When did you not realize you were being hilarious? What was everyone laughing about?

What's something you always thought was normal, but isn't?
When did you realize it wasn't?

_____

_____

_____

_____

_____

_____

What's one thing you believe in that no one can change your mind about,
evidence be dammed?

_____

_____

_____

_____

_____

_____

What's the best deed you've ever done anonymously?

_____

_____

_____

_____

_____

_____

Right this very minute, what's the biggest way you could disappoint someone?
Who would that person be?

To what relative are you most similar? Describe the similarities.

What color clothes do you wear most often? Spend 10 minutes free-form writing about what that color means for you, and why it shows up so often in your wardrobe.

What thing do you still think of as
"for grown-ups" and not for you—even though
you are a grown-up now?

You're compelled by law to get a word
or image tattooed on the palm of your hand.
What do you choose?

What law do you think should be repealed?

What's something people do that you think
should be outlawed?

You have one month to raise $5,000 in cash without your family
knowing. How do you go about it?

Who was your first teacher who wasn't a teacher?

Write about someone you remember quite vividly, but whom
you're sure doesn't remember you.

Imagine your favorite relative and your least favorite relative.
They're arguing about you. What do they say? Who wins?

Are you getting better or worse? Evidence?

What are/were your tricks for impressing a crush? Lay out your arsenal.

Write a job listing for your current job, making it sound as awesome as possible.

Write a note to the candidate who just got your job, telling them why it's the worst job in the world and they shouldn't even consider taking it.

Write a paragraph about your mother or father without using adjectives.

Describe—or imagine—the moment when your parents first met.

Of the people you dislike, who's most aware of your animosity?
Who's the most oblivious?

What's your inner age? Why'd you get stuck there?

When was the last time you were wrong?

How would your friends describe your personality? How would your family members describe it? What about strangers—the barista, the gas station attendant?

Your memoir is becoming a movie. Who should play you?
Describe the opening shot.

Write about the first time you remember using a computer. What were you doing, and what was your experience of it like?

What was the meanest thing somebody has said or done to you?

What is the meanest thing you've said or done to someone else?

Complete this sentence: "I wish I had _____."
Now write for another 10 minutes about why.

Your family has to enter the Witness Protection Program. Pick your new names and fictional background. Is it a story everyone in the family will keep straight? Which family member is going to give you away, and how?

Take us inside your grandmother's liquor cabinet.

The scariest thing is realizing that you are slowly turning into your parents.
What does that mean for you?

Who in your family tree are you named after, and why?
Who do you wish you were named after?

That girl/guy in high school that made you insanely jealous . . . what about them?

If you lived in the right era for you, what era would you live in?

A moment when you wanted to be older than you were.

A moment when you wanted to be younger than you were.

A moment when you were happy to be exactly the age you were.

When you were young, what would you have found if you dug around in
your mom's drawers, in those places she put things she hoped you
wouldn't find. What did you find, since surely you did that . . . ?

What are you in the middle of?

Seeing a double rainbow has nothing on that time you were struck with mind-bending, jaw-dropping awe. What did you see?

A time you've been lucky.

Something you've stolen.

What is your six-word memoir?

Pick an exotic celebration or holiday from some faraway place. Write about what happens when your family, for some reason, decides to observe that holiday.

If you asked your first enemy to describe you, what would she say.
What were the circumstances that made her your nemesis?

Write up the Rules of the House for your house.

What's the most consequential act of
your life? Good or bad.

Did you ever change your name?
Explain what happened.

What is the mental health diagnosis you
worry about most? Why?

Write the first line of your memoir.

You're a critic, reviewing the movie of your life. Write a thumbs-up review.
Now a thumbs-down one.

What you know of your family's history: all told, is it a gift to you or a curse?
Defend your argument.

List three people you consider enemies. Why so?

You get three do-overs. What would they be?

In your family, what's the unspoken way you make amends?

Describe what you sound like when you're angry. Take the perspective of someone in earshot behind a closed door, listening.

Write about a time that a parent gave you bad advice.

A time you've been ashamed of yourself.

That time you were bullied nearly to your breaking point.
What did you do? What didn't you do?

Make up a word you need but that doesn't exist, define it, and explain
why you need it.

What's the one letdown that you can't let go of?

Your earliest memory of being lost or separated from your parents.

What delighted you as a child? What disgusted you? Recreate a scene with you in it where you feel one of these ways.

Describe the one thing you wish you had said and the moment you wish you had said it.

That time you ran away from home.

Write the jacket copy
(brief cover description) for your memoir.

How would you be different if you had
grown up in great wealth?

You awake in fear in your childhood bed.
You just had a nightmare.
What did you dream about?

This is the one thing you'd change about
your best friend.

Describe an unexpected gift. One that didn't come in a brightly-wrapped package.

Describe one of your hidden talents and what it says about you.

Write a perfectly (and brutally, if necessary) honest valentine to your current or former love.

If you had siblings, did you fight with your siblings, and over what?

Write a secret message that only one other person will understand.
Explain how it came to be.

Tell the tale about a day that would never end.
Then write a haiku about one that flashed by.

The day you admitted to yourself that you did not love your siblings equally.

Be your own psychic. Write a snapshot of your future.

The last time you wet your bed (or a similar embarrassing involuntary act).

What's the worst idea that seemed like a good idea at the time?

The time you were jealous of your old best friend's new best friend.

Recount the first time you spent the night in a tree fort
(or other proudly-devised shelter).

Some believe we choose our parents. Write about why you would have chosen yours.

Now write about why you would not have chosen yours.

The time a person you thought you knew well stole from you.

That time you met one of your biggest childhood heroes.

The time you won something.

What's in the candy bar of You—what are the ingredients,
in what proportions? What is it called?

Write a list of specific dos and don'ts that will magically
be delivered to your teenage self.

Recreate the last conversation you had with a friend you no longer speak to.

What did you learn about life from your
favorite television character?

What are the three oddest characteristics
about you?

How would you be different if your first and
middle name were reversed?

What was the joke or prank that you wish
you never attempted?

Take us on a tour of your childhood home.

How did it feel to purchase your first car? Whatever happened to it?

Is there a next life? Write a scene in which you and at least one other person have strong and differing opinions on the matter. Don't just write a conversation/argument, everyone in the scene must want and need and act.

Write about your childhood home and family from the perspective of your pet. How did he/she experience your life there? Did your cat claw up the curtains when your dad came home? Did the goldfish mouth for food when your mother shimmied into the living room? If you didn't have a family pet, imagine one, e.g., "I'm the fart-firing, beef-jerky-addicted Boston Terrier X never had."

You're walking out the door after that critical first sleepover.
What are your thoughts and sensations?

What were your first signs of puberty?

What were your earliest moneymaking schemes?

What was your worst day traveling?

Why were you so bad at that one subject in school?

Allergies, medical conditions, overprotective parents: What set you physically apart?

What do you hate about where you grew up, and how do you deal with it?

Tell the story of the first dinner party you attended.

What are the top five mistakes your parents made that you've sworn not to repeat?

Describe your first purchase with your own money.

Your drivers' test: triumph or fiasco?

Write about the time you got kicked out of someplace/anyplace.

What is your strongest value: Courage? Honor? Loyalty? Honesty? Write a scene
that shows us your highest value in action, without once naming that value.

_____

_____

_____

_____

_____

_____

_____

_____

_____

_____

_____

_____

_____

_____

_____

_____

_____

_____

_____

_____

_____

_____

Write the story of naming your first pet, or not getting that pet but thinking up
the name you would have named if only . . .

Who is the one person you'd wish out of your life? Why? Write about how
you imagine your life immediately following this person's departure.

What would you most change about yourself? Write a scene in which that change in
yourself is realized. How are you and your world different?

What is it you most long for?
Write the scene where you're going after what you want.

Narrate one of your elementary-school daydreams.

What are you in a hurry to do today?

What are you in a hurry to do this year?

What are you in a hurry to do this decade?

Rant about a group you hate. Now write about them ranting back.

You are standing in front a group you hate. Persuade them to change their ways.

What's the meanest thing a stranger has
said to you? How did you react?

How would you describe your hometown
to a stranger in a foreign land?

When you were young, what skill or talent
came easily to you? How did it shape you?

What would be your worst nightmare?

There's another person inside you trying to get out. Write about that other person—who it is, what he or she would do if free, why you keep them trapped.

If you were a kid again, which game would you most want to play? Why?
Write the scene where you, as an adult, play that game again.

How did that one special book change your life?

You accidentally sent a sensitive text to the wrong person.
What ensued?

List 20 people you would be highly uncomfortable sitting next to on a plane.

You just got the worst haircut of your life.
Paint the scene and all your feelings.

Describe seeing the ocean for the first time.
. . . And the hundredth time.

List five favorite songs. Describe what you were doing
when you became hooked on each one.

Write about the midnight phone call you receive from an old
love, now single, who unceremoniously dumped you 10 years ago.
Or the emotional equivalent.

From family stories you've been told, describe the life of a
great-grandparent or other deceased relation.

You've been granted your wish to be the celebrity you've fantasized about being,
for a day. Describe that day.

What's the first thing you remember being
afraid of as a kid?
How did you conquer that fear?

What was in your treasure box when you
were a child?

What fad of your youth didn't live up
to the hype?

Ever try to assemble/build/create something
without (or ignoring) the instructions?
What happened?

Imagine yourself in another century and place. Where would you go? Why?
Write a scene that places you there, that compares and contrasts where
you are with where you've left.

How did that one food become so nostalgic for you?

Remember when you got that terrible rash? Tell the story.

Write the toast you'd give at your parents' divorce.

Write about the object that meant the most to you as a kid.

Write the refrain to a country music song about your brother
(or someone you consider a brother).

Has anyone significantly younger developed an obsessive crush on you?
Describe the situation.

Pick three pivotal, historical happenings in your lifetime. Now recall where you were when you heard about them, what you thought of the moment then, and what you think of its significance now.

What are your personal superstitions? How did they come to be?

Relive a moment in your past—but give it an outcome different from the one that occurred. Make the new result as different (but as logical) as possible.

"Nothing ever happens on Tuesdays." Write about when it did.

Write about the time you got lost. Where did you end up? Where did
you need to get to? How did you get out of it and find your way
again? How did the experience reduce or enrich you?

Were you ever someone's second choice? When did you become aware of this?

Have you ever done anything to make yourself seem more intelligent? How did that work out?

If bragging were socially acceptable, what would you brag about?

"No fair!" is a child's common complaint. But what was truly unfair about your childhood?

The author Cheryl Strayed had to walk 2,650 miles from Mexico to Canada over the Sierra Mountains to find herself. What did you have to do?

Your boss has just told you to do something that you know will embarrass both of you, badly. Write about what happens next.

Describe a time when a stranger thought you were someone else.

You are a toy. In three scenes, write about who makes you,
who buys you, who keeps you.

What was your worst babysitting experience?
Write the inner dialogue for the baby and sitter.

Write about when you were in physical danger.

You meet your identical twin, from whom you were separated at birth.
Your twin grew up in circumstances dramatically different from your own.
How are you different and similar?

Write about the object you think will mean the most to you at the end of your days.

Write about the object that means the most to you now.

Describe the moment you were caught in a snowstorm, hurricane, or pouring rain.

Describe your last visit to see a dying relative.

_____

_____

_____

_____

_____

_____

_____

_____

_____

Write about a vacation that went really, really wrong.

_____

_____

_____

_____

_____

_____

_____

_____

_____

_____

Write an open-letter response to claims your memoir is a fraud.

Persuade the powers that be to change that one rule.

If you could throw a celebration for someone in your past, what would it be like?

What is the best thing that happened to you today? This week?
This year?

You are looking through your mother's purse as a child.
What do you find?

Catalogue yourself as a physical specimen at the age of 14.
Include descriptions of posture, gestures, tics, and other physical mannerisms.

Describe the backyard of your youth (or the functional equivalent).
Tell us about an unforgettable moment you spent there.

What are your rules of physical attraction?
Have they changed over the years?

What's the most you've ever spent on a night
on the town? Was it worth it?

What was your biggest failure?
Did you have to struggle with feeling that
it made you a failure?

What didn't happen, but you wish did?

What lies or half-truths did your parents
tell you, just to get you to behave?

When was your trust misplaced?

What haven't you tried yet, despite suspecting
that you'd enjoy it?

What joke would you like to teach a
five-year-old? Who taught that joke to you?

If you could only have 10 ingredients to eat for the rest of your life (and forget about nutrition here), what would they be? Describe each ingredient—when you started eating it, your strongest memory of eating it, what you like to cook with it.

Write a diary entry for the best day you've never had.

Write a letter describing yourself to a grandparent you never knew.

Tell us about your favorite food—its look, taste, smell, and feel. What does that food do to you physically and emotionally? Who and what does it represent? What are the memories it triggers? Show us all this in a scene—a scene where you want, but can't get to, your favorite food.

Write a diary entry for the worst day you've never had.

_____

_____

_____

_____

_____

_____

_____

_____

_____

Retell a family story about your childhood. Did it really happen that way?

_____

_____

_____

_____

_____

_____

_____

_____

_____

List six things you want to do before your next birthday.

Describe who you are now, from an older-self's perspective.

What did you learn about work from your first job that turned out
to be absolutely true? (Or false. You choose.)

What was your favorite piece of clothing as a child,
and what story does that piece of clothing tell?

Write about that time you dressed up in costume—for Halloween, for theater,
for make-believe. Describe the costume in detail, and the occasion, and how it
made you feel; and how it felt to get out of the costume and go back to your
regular clothes.

Describe a time when you overheard your parents or other people in your family fighting. What was it about? How did you feel? What was the outcome?

Do you recall a meal that completely changed your perspective or mood? Describe that meal in its sensual detail.

What is your favorite accessory: a hat? Tattoo? Jewelry? Monocle? Prosthetic? Gold tooth? What does it mean to you? Write about how the accessory makes you feel when you wear it. Write about how you feel without it.

Ever taken a trip and ended up somewhere completely unexpected? How did that come about? How did the trip turn out?

Describe yourself at three different ages. In the last two, explain how your younger versions are still contained within your older self.

If you were an animal, which animal would you be? Why?
Write a scene from your animal point of view.

You had a secret hiding spot in the house where you used to live. When do you
go there? What do you bring? What does this place look like from the inside?
From the outside? Were you ever discovered?

Write about the one thing you never did and desperately regret.

Write about any place you've called home—but write about the
period before it felt like home.

Explain what it felt like to break up with someone you loved.

You invite a childhood friend you haven't seen in years to come
visit you. He or she shows up, and they're still the same age.
Describe your dinner conversation.

Choose one word to be erased from everyone's memory—for the sole purpose of making your life better.

What's the worst thing you've ever wished on someone?

Does the future excite or frighten you? Why?

What habit did you intentionally cultivate? Which one did you struggle to drop?

What is it you most long for? Write the scene where you get it.

What is it you most long for? Write the scene where you know you'll never get it.

You are a small child noticing something in nature for the first time. Maybe it's a squirrel outside or the little veins on the face of a leaf or ants crawling on the sidewalk. How does this discovery make you feel?

Persuade us to like that thing that you like. (Specifically, that thing you like that no one else does.)

Your life is a TV show, and today is the last episode of the season: What would be the cliffhanger that you end with to get people to tune in next season?

What is/was it like to go shopping with your mother?

What's something you said to a family member that you wish you could take back, and why did you say it at the time?

Using all your senses, describe your favorite season of the year.

Write a series of Post-it notes to your 80-year-old self, instructing them to do something you know they won't want to do (and have perhaps forgotten how).

Write the dialogue for the strangest conversation you've overheard in a public restroom.

Jay-Z has New York, Bruce Springsteen's got Asbury Park, Edith Piaf Paris. . . . If you were to pay musical tribute to a place that made you who you are (for better or worse), where would that be? Write that song.

Write the biography for a piece of clothing that was given to you.

List your teachers from kindergarten through senior year of high school if you can.
What would they remember about you?

When did someone give you surprisingly useful inside information?

What was your most instructive mistake?

What mistake would you gladly make all over again?

What do you dislike about other members of your own gender?

Describe a circumstance that seemed terrible at the time but
turned out for the best in the end.

Write about a promise that you didn't keep.

What is your worst character trait? Is it something you've tried to
change over the years, or accepted and managed about yourself?

Write 20 sentences describing your life. The first word in each sentence must alternate between "Fortunately" and "Unfortunately."

Describe your most serious physical injury, beginning with the
healing process and working backward.

Choose three personal items and write an accompanying letter
to put into a time capsule that will be opened in 100 years.

Life isn't comprised solely of major life-changing events—there's a lot of drag time. Think of a time when you were deeply bored. What were you doing? Maybe it was repetitive work, a long vacation with relatives, or being stuck in a place you didn't like. Write about soul-crushing, brain-numbing boredom. Then look deeper. Was there anything good about the boredom?

The worst time your parent/guardian punished you. Write the scene from his/her point of view. Go as deep and as honest as you can, and then push further.

Write the dialogue for a heated argument you had that still feels unresolved.

If you could turn back time and run for president of your high school student body, what would your platform be? Your campaign slogan? Would you be a shoe-in, or would the old school president still win?

Write about that present that was a huge disappointment.

Describe a challenge you overcame as a child, and how you did it.

No one else's family is like yours. How do they stand out from others?

Take a funny episode from your life and rewrite it as a tragedy, or vice versa.

What's the most embarrassing thing you've done to impress a boyfriend/girlfriend? How did the other person respond?

You're having a fight with your father (or mother, or uncle, or cousin).
No one is shouting but the tension is smoldering hotly. What do you say?
How does he or she respond? What happens next?

Can you remember a moment that was a turning point in a relationship,
whether with a sibling, friend, or lover? Write about that moment and
what led up to it.

Describe a time you almost got into a fight.

Write about what recess was like in elementary school.

You are closer to one parent than the other. Why is that?

You've decided to place a phrase, in needlepoint, on the wall in your living room. Pick that phrase.

Is there anything about a younger generation that inspires genuine envy in you?

You've hired an advertising agency to write a slogan for the brand of You. What do they come up with?

Before you learned the truth about sex, where did you think babies came from?

What was the worst job you ever had? Did you have to wear a uniform? Describe what your duties were there and what you looked like as you were working there.

You feel a lust so unstoppable that you think your clothes might spontaneously combust. Write about the object of that lust.

You wake up with a vague feeling of dread. Search through all the things
that make you anxious to figure out what is bothering you.

Think of a decade in your life and the soundtrack you would create
for that decade—the songs and musicians. Why that music, and what
did it say about who you were then?

Write about an evening at your home from the perspective of your cat.

Describe the last fight you had with your mother. Use dialogue.

Describe the first house you lived in, and how it looked to you
if you ever saw it when you were older.

Do you talk about matters with your female friends differently than with
your male ones? Describe a subject that the genders treated differently.

Describe getting lost while surfing the Internet.
Where do you end up?

What does "home" smell like? Where is "home"? Have you been there recently?

Describe the activity or adventure that you'd like to have again.

List the authors/books that best represent your life stages (briefly, e.g., "My life, from Maurice Sendak to Jack Kerouac to David Brooks to . . .").

Do the same with music (briefly, e.g., "Songs of myself: Barney to Brahms to Beyoncé").

_____

_____

_____

_____

_____

_____

Write about something you tend to or care for that's important to you.

_____

_____

_____

_____

_____

_____

What's the most trouble you've ever landed in?
Describe the consequences or how you got out of it.

_____

_____

_____

_____

_____

_____

Describe a dream you had. Use language designed to sell the story to Hollywood.

At the end of a phone call, you realize the friend you were talking to forgot
to hang up; and you overhear him disparaging you to whomever he was with.
Describe what you overhear, and what happens.

What did you resist doing
for the longest time?

Describe your most revealing
aha moment—your revelatory breakthrough
in understanding.

Describe an aspect of your life you wish
you could be more relaxed about.
Why aren't you?

When did you unintentionally
frighten someone?

Was there a character in a book you wanted to be when you were young? Write a story where that character is in your life, like Jo March growing up where you did, at the time you did.

You can read people's minds at will.
Among your family and friends, whose mind
will you intentionally never probe?

What have you technically outgrown,
but still enjoy doing?

Describe the last holiday when you were alone
(but didn't want to be).

Describe every place you have lived,
in one word. Then do it again with a verb.

Write a video-game scene in which you are the central character, either hero or villain. Really bring this video world to life—and your character, and those around you, and the rules and objective of the game.

Read the label of your favorite junk food and look up something about each ingredient. Now write a letter to the company that makes the product.

Describe your childhood bedroom. Include at least three senses.

Describe the last time you kissed someone. But instead of describing the physical aspects, describe it in terms of the feelings you and the other person felt each step of the way.

Write about a time when you taught someone how to do something new.

Write about a peculiar skill, quirk, obsession of yours that's most likely to land you in the book of Guinness World Records.

Describe the time in your life you felt most heroic.

What did you want to be when you were 12 years old? Did you
stick to it; and, if not, what changed your course? If you
did, delve into moments that tested your conviction.

Why did you dread that certain class? How did you cope?

Write about the last major dilemma you faced. Do you think you
made the right choice? Did the experience change your view of
life, yourself, your work, your world?

If you're at home, reach over to the drawer closest to where
you are right now, and write about each object in the drawer,
conveying its meaning to you.

Among the goals you haven't achieved, which ones are no longer
possible? Write a retirement ceremony for them.

What's the most difficult thing you ever discussed with your parents?
Write the conversation from your parents' perspective.

What's the most convoluted way you ever tried to get out of doing something?
Did it succeed? If so, at what price?

It turns out life's a game show. To make it to the next level, you
get to call one friend. Who do you call? Describe that conversation.

Remember that amazing first date? Take us on it with you.

_____

_____

_____

_____

_____

_____

Describe that awful first date. What did it teach you?

_____

_____

_____

_____

_____

_____

Describe a moment when you felt betrayed by someone close to you.

_____

_____

_____

_____

_____

_____

Write an e-mail to someone you decided to stop speaking to. Describe the incident (final straw) that prompted you to stop speaking to them. Explain why you decided to cut them out of your life. You don't have to be nice. But try to be clear, honest, and precise.

Write a text message to a younger you with the best advice you've ever received.
How would this younger you respond? Let the conversation play out and see where
any tension lies.

That moment when you were convinced you were going to fail, but you succeeded.

Write the real job description for your first job.

You broke the law and got away with it. What was your plan if you'd gotten caught?

Who is someone in your life who'd you'd like to be for a day? Describe that day.

_____

_____

_____

_____

_____

_____

_____

_____

_____

Recall a conversation when you meant to say one thing but it came out all wrong.

_____

_____

_____

_____

_____

_____

_____

_____

_____

Joan Didion writes: "It is easy to see the beginnings of things, and harder to see the ends." Write about the beginning of something and how it ended.

Describe a perfectly average day when something extraordinary happened.

Write about that time someone rubbed you the wrong way,
for reasons you're still not sure of today.

Write about an object you own that you'd never sell, and why you wouldn't.

Have you experienced unrequited love? When and how did
you let yourself realize it was unrequited?

Write about a day when technology (e-mail, your phone, computer, or text) failed you. Show, don't tell.

Write about a black sheep in your family history.

What is it like not to be
invited to a party?

What is the mistake you keep repeating
over and over?

Write a grocery list of your
current emotions.

Describe the last time you cried,
and why.

Tell a story of something you regret doing. Make it a comedy.

Remember when you were small and played hide-and-seek? Imagine yourself as a small child, hiding. What thoughts are passing through your mind? What are you wearing? What does it feel like to be inside your body?

Have you ever developed an obsessive crush on someone significantly different in age—much younger or older? What did you do about it?

What was the thing you coveted most as a child, and why. What happened when you did or didn't get it?

What are the objects from childhood that you still hang on to, and why those particular ones? If you haven't held on to anything, why not?

Describe a bad day (but with humor) solely in a series of a Facebook status updates.

Tweet an original thought and quote yourself. Use the hashtag #642things.

The time you didn't see it coming.

What is the best present you ever got from a friend?

What kept you up last night?

You've just been given a budget of $250,000 by a toy company
to create a new toy. Tell us what you do.

You're awarded a lifetime supply of anything you choose—but the catch
is you have to store that supply in your home and carry it with you
when you move. What do you choose?

Write about losing enthusiasm. What were you once mad about
doing? How did that interest fade?

Write about a disappointing moment when you were a child.
Then write about a similar moment when you were a teenager.
Then write about such a moment now.

Describe your life as a mythological struggle.
What mighty deeds will they ascribe to you a thousand years from now?

There's always a birthday that just goes wrong—a misguided celebration, a surprise that hits you the wrong way, a completely forgotten birthday, et cetera. Think back on that day: What were the specific details that made it so horrible? It's your birthday, and you can cry if you want to!

The Seven Deadly Sins are pride, anger, gluttony, lust, envy, sloth, and greed. Whether you believe in them as sins or not, write about a time when one of these feelings got the better of you and you acted in a less than angelic way.

What subject in school do you wish you had continued studying?
How would that have changed your life?

Write about the person who you hope you never see again.
Ever.

Write about how you envision your last day on the job—the day you retire from working. If you're already retired, write about the circumstances under which you'd unretire.

What hobby have you never gotten around to taking up,
but you think you'd enjoy? What's stopped you?

You open the door and in front of you stands your twin,
who you never knew of. Describe what happens next.

Write about a comical misunderstanding: that song lyric you
misheard, that advice you took too literally, et cetera.

Think of a moment in your life that you'd like to write about. Close your eyes, and put yourself back in that moment. Now write about everything except the actual action of the moment itself: What was the weather like? What kinds of sounds were there around you? Were there any smells? What was the room like where you were (or the outdoors, if you were outsides)? What other action was going on around you? Write down every single thing you remember about the surroundings, so that if a set designer had to recreate it (including smells and touch), they'd have the needed blueprints.

Write about a time you lied or cheated and felt terrible about it.
And then, write about a time you felt no remorse.

The politics of people around us often change. As the times change, things once less acceptable by many become more socially acceptable. Think of someone you know who has changed his or her mind about a political issue. Write about the transformation.

Did anyone ever give you a gift as a sign of their love? From a ring that comes out of a gumball machine to a special book they bought for you, the objects that people give us may have deep emotional significance. Think of something that was given to you as a gift and how it made you feel.

Have you ever had a nickname? When was the last time someone called you that?
(If you've never had a nickname, pick one for yourself.)

What's the snappiest comeback you've ever unleashed? Tell that story.

What's the biggest tip you've ever left? Were you trying to
impress someone, or were you rewarding extraordinary service?
Tell that story.

Name a time you were funny and
everyone laughed.

What was true when you were younger
but isn't now?

What is one thing you keep forgetting to do?
Write about it.

Did you ever have a coincidence in
your life that made you believe in fate?

If you could erase one moment from your life, which one would it be? Why?

What are all the things that would be different about your life today if you erased that moment? What would not have happened (good things as well as bad)?

Were you raised with any religious rituals? If so, write about a ritual
that was carried out and how it made you feel. If there were no religious
rituals, write about a ritual of family life that was always carried out
the same way in your family.

Did your family have enough money when you were growing up? If they struggled to
make ends meet, how did you feel about it? If you had more than others, how did
that make you feel?

Someone has sat you down to talk to you about sex. Maybe it's your mother or the health teacher or your older cousin. Now you are nervously listening. What do they tell you? What do they get wrong that it will take you a long time to figure out?

Several versions of the Buddha's life hold that he began as a wealthy prince, protected from seeing poverty and death as a child, who then wandered out of the palace one day and saw the suffering of the dying and the poor. When did you first wander outside and see the suffering of the world?

Write about the best time someone touched you (in a non-intimate way).

When have you experienced double standards? Have you imposed any yourself?

When did you become aware of your race? Was it a positive or negative experience?

Name the five biggest "almosts" in your life.

What's the most likely scenario that would cause you and your significant other to
go your separate ways?

Describe your daily "unwinding" routine when you were 10.
Compare and contrast with the one you have today.

Interview yourself for five minutes. Ask the hard questions.

Imagine your life as an opera. In an opera, the highs are high and
the lows are low. What kind of costumes are the characters wearing?
What would be the aria that the lead is singing? When the tragedy
happens, as it inevitably does, what is the theme?

You can send one message that's guaranteed to be anonymous, and never traced back to you. Who do you send it to? What's the message?

In your youth, who was the funniest person you knew?
Do you think you'd still find them funny today?

You walk into a place, order "the usual," and get it.
What kind of place is it? What have you just ordered?

Have you ever felt like an outsider in your own family?
Write a scene that shows that.

Pick two romantic relationships from your past—people who didn't know each other.
Imagine them as roommates. How would they get along?

It's the day after your first kiss.
A song is running through your head.
What is it?

What did your mother tell you
about her mother?

Ever make up your own original game,
as a child or as an adult?
What were the rules?

Have you ever completely changed a habit;
and what inspired you to do so?

Make a list of 10 things from your life that you would never write about in a
million years. Start writing about one of them.

Write about a time you got in over your head.

When did you first experience hypocrisy?

Were you ever a go-between for others—secret lovers, enemies, estranged relatives? What did the experience teach you?

Describe a place where you felt unsafe as a child, and why.

Describe yourself as a flavor of ice cream, making up any flavor you'd like.

Growing up, what games did you play with other kids?

What does your collection of books, and how you keep them, say about you?

Imagine yourself in a family therapy session. What would the therapist
say to each of you? How would that scene go?

What class in school was most frustrating to you, and why?
Describe a scene from that class.

When didn't you stick up for someone when you should have?
Describe the scene and how you felt later.

Describe a fight you had with someone, then rewrite it
from the other person's point of view.

Write about the time you thought someone was kidding (they weren't).

What's the quickest way to make you angry—the shortcut path to pushing your buttons? If someone were deliberately trying to do that, how would they behave?

What are the stereotypes about someone like you? Which of those do you consider offensive? Which do you think have grains of truth?

Think about the most picked-on, loser kid in high school.
Put yourself in that kid's head and write about a typical
day in school.

Think about the most popular kid in high school.
Put yourself in his or her head and describe the
scene at lunch.

What is a family secret that was revealed to you at some point?
Why do you think it was kept secret?
Why was it revealed to you at that particular time?

Who is your frenemy? Why?

When did you feel the most attractive
in your life?

When were you the most frightened
in the outdoors?

Was there ever something you weren't allowed
to have because of your gender?

Write about a time when your behavior shocked and embarrassed you, but write about it from the third person, being as objective as you can about what happened.

What was the place outdoors that always felt like your special place? Have you ever returned there, and how had it changed?

Did you ever get in trouble and get sent to the principal of the
school (or reprimanded by a similar authority figure)?
What did you do to try to get them to let you off easy?

If you weren't doing the work you do now, if you had taken
an entirely different career path, what would that career be?
Imagine what it would be like.

Have you ever realized you were addicted to something?
How did you deal with it?

Have you ever been (or almost been) the victim of a scam?
When did you get wise?

What's your history with obscenities? When did you first learn them?
When have you used them?

You have three years to achieve full-fledged mastery in something.
Write about the skill you choose, and how you'd go about it.

Now you have six months to become the world's greatest expert in something.
What do you choose? What's your strategy?

When did a teacher open your eyes about something? Write about that epiphany.

What did you do that backfired?

Describe five ways in which you're hopelessly old-fashioned.

A camera of the future allows you to see—live—whatever you want,
whenever you want. Describe what you decide to watch.

If you could go back to one moment (one time/one place) in your life, and live
there for the rest of your life, what moment would it be? Why?

Recall an evening when you walked by and peeked in the window of a stranger's house.

Tell us about the time someone broke your heart. And then did it again.

What job would you have been most suited for 400 years ago? Describe an imaginary workday that best displays how you'd give the work your personal touch.

What popular tourist destination would you never like to visit?
Now write about visiting there.

What city do you most identify with, and why?

Who's the one who got away?

Tell us something that doesn't make any sense about you. Not one bit of sense.

If asked, how would your first love describe you?

Describe your first computer—the feel of your fingers on the keyboard, its look and model.

List five people you love and five others you used to love.

Name six ways you are resilient.

Write about the last city you fell in love with.

Explain why you didn't keep that secret.

That moment when someone said "I love you" and you didn't say it back.

Imagine someone who has harmed you in the past calling to make amends.
How would the conversation go?

Tell a story from one of your grandparents' point of view.

Describe a conversation with yourself about whether or not to have children.

What is the thing in life that you have been most addicted to, and why is it that substance (or person, or behavior)? Have your addictions changed?

Tell the story about a time you said something you didn't mean.

Write about the thing that you thought was a secret,
but which everyone around you knew full well.

The moment you missed your train, plane, or bus.
What happened next?

What is a recurring dream you keep having? Write it.

Put on your favorite song and write down what comes to mind.

Describe falling off a bike in 100 words or less.

Whose death in your life hit you hardest, and how did you cope
with the situation over the next month?

Everyone is full of contradictions. What are some of yours?
Pick something contradictory about yourself and write about it.

Imagine you could spend a day in another town with another identity. Describe going
to a coffee house there and interacting with people as that new person.

_____

_____

_____

_____

_____

_____

_____

_____

_____

_____

_____

_____

_____

_____

_____

_____

_____

_____

_____

_____

_____

Being 10 is powerful. A whole decade of life under your belt.
Imagine yourself at 10. You look in the mirror and say something
to yourself. What do you say?

_____

_____

_____

_____

_____

_____

When did you first realize you were a girl or a boy? How did you feel about it?
Was there ever a time when you wanted to be a different gender or playacted
being another gender?

_____

_____

_____

_____

_____

_____

_____

How were girls treated differently from boys in your family?
Write how it felt from your gender perspective to watch how
the other gender was treated.

_____

_____

_____

_____

_____

_____

Your mother's jewelry box: You're looking through it. She's said you can have one thing, anything you want. Describe this object using at least three senses. What made you choose it?

At what point in your life did you feel that you had discovered your purpose, and how successful have you been in fulfilling that sense of purpose?

What is something that you are completely untalented at? Is there a reason that you feel you have no talent in that direction—were you ever discouraged, or did you never have a chance to explore them?

When was a time that you had to ask someone for money? Maybe it was your mother or a friend or relative or even a complete stranger. How did it feel to be in that situation?

A classic children's story is "The Ugly Duckling." The duckling thinks he is the ugliest bird around, but then discovers he's a swan. Was there a trait of yours that you thought was terrible that turned out to be a strength?

You are with a boyfriend or girlfriend on your last date ever with them. You eat Chinese food; and when you crack open the fortune cookie, the slip of paper seems to summarize your whole relationship. What does it say?

Someone in your family or neighborhood is missing, maybe for an hour, maybe for years. What happened?

Other than emergency supplies, pets, and family members, what are the items you would carry out of your house if there were an earthquake or fire and you could only take what you could grab quickly?

Describe the outfit that is most characteristically you, and why.

Write about a situation in which you had to do something against your will.

What does your dream house look like?

You are on the dance floor and feeling pretty good about your moves.
Describe how it feels to be in your body. What music are you listening
to? Who is checking you out?

Your parent has a bad habit, an odd habit. You wonder if other people notice.
Go ahead and write about it. You don't need to show anyone.

What book did you entirely get lost in? Write about the main character
as if he or she were your friend.

Write a scene on a train with a stranger you find attractive.

Did you ever do something terrible that someone forgave you for?
Describe that.

You're sitting at the Thanksgiving table next to one of your most eccentric relatives. Describe this person to us—what does he or she look like, smell like, sound like? What makes him or her eccentric? You two begin to talk. Write the dialogue of that conversation. What happens when it's silent; or is silence not allowed?

What body part of yours do people comment on most? How does
that make you feel? What are your stock responses?

Imagine if you had married your first boyfriend or girlfriend.
How would things be different now?

Write a scene where the weather matches your mood.

Write about a time you were in the wilderness, using as much sensory detail
as possible.

Remember the last time you didn't get your wish, and how you felt about it,
and what eventually happened.

"You can do it!" someone is yelling. Who's yelling? Why are they yelling this? Where are you?

Describe a time you experienced déjà vu.

Describe a time you yelled at a stranger.

Who taught you how to ride a bicycle? Why that person? Describe this bicycle, the paint, color, bicycle seat, wheels. What happened when the other person let go?

You're standing in front of your first car. Tell us what it looks like. Open the door and get in. Describe the interior, the dashboard and steering wheel, the radio, the seats. What's that on the floor? How does it feel to sit in this car? Where are you going?

You can hear a song coming from the house or apartment next door. Who's playing it—or who do you imagine is playing it? What words can you make out? What can't you hear? What is it about this song that won't let you go?

You're a kid, and it's the hottest day ever. Where do you go to escape the heat?
Who else is with you; or are you alone? What surprising thing happens?

_____

_____

_____

_____

_____

_____

_____

_____

_____

_____

_____

_____

_____

_____

_____

_____

_____

_____

_____

_____

_____

Have you ever had a secret admirer? Write about finding out who
it was.

Describe something you already know you'll never do again, no
matter how long you live.

Write about a time when you felt excluded from a group.

Write about a time when friends pressured you to do something
you really didn't want to do.

Apologize to someone for something in the past that you never
apologized for.

You're a kid. Your mother leans over to kiss you good-bye.
What does she smell like? What does her skin feel like?
Where is she going?

What is the first book you remember? Tell us how the pages felt
and what they smelled like. Did someone read this book to you,
or did you read it to yourself? Where was this?

How tall are you? What's terrific about that height? What about it sucks?
If you could, what would change about it?

Where is an ancestor of yours buried? Why there? What does
their gravestone look like? (Or: What do you imagine it looks
like?) If there's no gravestone, tell us about that, too.

You're putting together a personal time capsule. Tell us about the objects you decide to put inside. How do these objects represent who you are at this moment of your life? You can also write one sentence and put it inside. What is it?

What is the most dramatic thing any of your siblings
(or other family member) has ever done?

Describe the first time you saw a member of the opposite sex naked.

What is your earliest memory of someone outside your family?

What is your first memory of visiting a foreign country?

Was there ever anyone you might have had a relationship with
if the timing hadn't been off?

Did you have an undeserved reputation in your family—say, for being
the clumsy one, when in fact you turned out to be graceful?

What year in your life was especially important? Maybe it's the year you graduated from high school, or when you traveled the world, got married, divorced, or retired. Write down 10 (or more) things you remember about that year, beginning each memory with "I remember. . . . " Close your eyes and randomly put your finger on one memory. Describe that memory in the minutest of detail.

Something is tapping on your window. Who or what is it? Do you go to it?
What happens when you do?

What's the greatest party you've ever been to? Where was it held? Who was there?
Tell us about the music, the food, the decorations.

Describe a time when you pretended to have a good time.

Describe a lie you told to make someone else feel better.

What is your secret vice? How do you justify it?

What was your most successful attempt
to scare someone?

What do you do when no one's looking?

What excuse are you still giving yourself?

When have you felt most free?

Who gave you your first name? What is its significance? If you're named after someone, tell us about their importance to your family. How are you like this person? Unlike them?

_____

_____

_____

_____

_____

_____

_____

_____

_____

_____

_____

_____

_____

_____

_____

_____

_____

_____

_____

What do you know about—really know a lot about? How did you become an expert in this area? In what ways, for all your expertise, are you still learning?

Tell us about the first job you had outside your family. How did this job come about? What exactly did you do? What is your current work? How are the two jobs connected?

You're in trouble, deep trouble. How did this come about?
Who found you out? What happened next?

List the languages you speak (at any level) and how you learned them. Feel free
to think broadly, including professional languages, the language of a sport,
cultural languages, digital languages, et cetera.

To which groups do you belong, and how big a role
do they play in your sense of self?

Think about a situation when you were itching to express yourself but had
to hold your tongue. Now let yourself rant.

How is your sense of humor different now from when you were younger?

Write about at time when you were too hard on yourself.

What is the most radical thing you've ever done to change your appearance, and why?

Imagine you're writing out a list of chores for the holidays.
Who gets assigned what? Justify your choices.

Write about your morning routine in precise detail, including
what gives you a sense of calm and what makes you frantic.

Pull out a photo of the oldest relative you know, as an adult or as a child. (This person may or may not be living.) Tell us everything you know about this person, what he or she looks like, the relation to you, everything. Where did he or she come from? What was the occasion of this photo? (If you don't know, feel free to imagine.) How is this person like or unlike you?

Have you ever found out something shocking about a friend that
changed the way you thought of her or him?

Describe a time when you were trying to help a situation and
ended up making it a lot worse.

Did you ever rat on someone? What happened?

Was there ever someone in your life you disliked at first and
then began to quite like? What changed your opinion?

What was a talent you believed you had as a kid that no one else noticed?
Or as an adult?

Describe how you have reacted in a crisis.

Describe a memorable road trip, in a car, bus, or train. When was this? Who's with you—or are you alone? Was there an urgency to arrive at your destination, or did you have all the time in the world? Tell us about a stranger you met along the way.

Set the timer on your phone for one minute. Write down all the secrets you know, big and small. Pick one and write about it.

The story starts: "It's not every day someone walks into your life to flip the whole thing upside down, which is why I'll always remember the moment I met . . . "
Write the rest.

Write about a time when you had to navigate a new culture, and what
you learned about yourself doing so, both good and not so good.

If you had to write a letter of apology, who might it be addressed to?
Write this letter.

Describe a time you completely changed your mind about something.

What was the most embarrassing thing someone you were with did,
and how did you react?

Was there a moment when you began to accept a part of your body
that you had never liked before?

Write a hypothetical dialogue between your online/digital persona(s) and your real self. This can be in the form of a conversation, IM, text . . .

The first time someone who you really respected told you that you were wrong

What event irrevocably altered your life, but you didn't know it at the time?

What lesson did you learn too late?

What family trait did you completely deny having as a child, but now admit is part of you?

Write about a time you blamed someone else for something you did.

What characteristic behavior do you most want to give up?
What would it take?

Who or what have you left behind? How did that happen?
Would you go back and change this if you could?

Guide a reader though the stamps in your passport, filling in stories, describing surprises about each trip, who you met, and what you hope will come next.

Describe the quality of yours you hope to pass on to your children
(or someone you've guided/helped raise). Describe the one you hope
they don't inherit.

You're having brunch with a girlfriend. Tell her about the last big
fight you had with your spouse, your partner, or your parents.

Write about the first time you were in a position of authority and how you felt
about it (scared, excited, apathetic). What did you do with that first power?

Is there a person in your life who is habitually late or compulsively on time?
What bothers you about this? Go ahead—rant.

Describe the absolutely worst present you've received.
Who gave it to you? What were their intentions?

Describe an area in your life where you feel like an outsider
and how you've learned to navigate this.

Write about something you can't let go of, even though it has
outlived its role in your life.

Write about something you keep private/hidden, be it in your
sock drawer or under your bed, or an emotion you hold in.

Write about a recurring argument you have with your sibling(s)
or closest friend and the origin of that tension.

You attend your high school reunion and someone says,
"Remember that time we did . . . " Who said that?
And what would be the story they would tell?

The opposite of déjà vu is jamais vu—experiencing a familiar thing as something
absolutely new. Has that happened in your life? If not, what moment would you pick
for an attack of jamais vu?

Write a how-to-guide to an area of your life where you're an expert
with examples from your own experiences.

For the longest time, you didn't realize you were doing it wrong.
Describe what "it" was and how you learned of your mistake.

Who is the most important person in your life? Why?

If you were made executive director of a charitable foundation,
what would be your three top causes, and why?

Describe the first time you mourned the death of someone (or of a pet).

Write about a significant time when you felt you had to
stand up to authority and protest.

Write about a time you changed your mind (and surprised yourself you did).

Name the person in your life who's least like you. How did you meet?
What kept you bonded?

Do you believe all people are fundamentally equal? Why or why not?

Write about when you became aware of yourself on the political spectrum.

Map out a defining journey in your life, from a trip to your alma mater for a college reunion to your morning commute. Briefly consider why you embarked on this journey and what you wanted, its obstacles, how you've overcome them or were defeated.

_____

_____

_____

_____

_____

_____

_____

_____

_____

_____

_____

_____

_____

_____

_____

_____

_____

_____

_____

_____

_____

Describe a pleasant experience with a less-than-pleasant aftermath.

Write about someone you feel like you should love, but you don't.

Write about the hardest thing you've ever had to ask for.

....

....

....

....

....

....

If you had to sum up your life-to-date as proof of an adage,
what would it be? Why?

....

....

....

....

....

What's your oldest fear, and when did you first experience it?

....

....

....

....

....

....

The first thing people notice about
my face is _____.

I'm far more _____
than people suspect.

If I ever go to prison,
it will be for _____.

Best gift you've ever received:
Why so meaningful and memorable?

Write a letter addressed to an object you've learned to live without (lost, sold, neglected . . .), telling this particular item why you're better off anyway.

How well can you recreate your family tree from memory? Write down or sketch as much as you can. In what ways does your family tree play a role in your life?

What's the last item of news that made you sign a petition,
donate to a cause, or write your congressman/congresswoman?
What made you respond?

What's the best thing you've ever done for the wrong reasons?

What's the worst thing you've done for the right reasons?

Using the format of the popular travel column "36 Hours" featured in the New York Times (which offers a model itinerary for 36 hours in a particular place), write a travel piece for your hometown about what to do there in that time period.

What is on your bucket list?

_____

_____

_____

_____

_____

_____

_____

_____

_____

Your friends at the San Francisco Writers' Grotto have asked you to add a 643rd writing prompt to this book. What's your contribution?

_____

_____

_____

_____

_____

_____

_____

_____

_____

_____

Do you believe in happily ever after? Why or why not?

What is your pet peeve? What was it 10 years ago?

Who do you envy, and why?

If you were a superhero, who would you be?

_____

_____

_____

_____

_____

_____

Who is your favorite villain?

_____

_____

_____

_____

_____

_____

If you won $5 million in a lottery, how would you spend it?

_____

_____

_____

_____

_____

_____

Imagine someone describing you to a blind person (who, understandably, isn't interested in facial features). How would they paint a non-visual portrait of you?

List the bad habits you've kicked. Next, write a to-do list of
the ones you've yet to conquer.

Write down the recipes for your favorite (and strangest) home remedies.
How did you pick these up?

What did you convince yourself was the plan all along?

If you were attending a potluck dinner, what dish would you take along?

What's the nicest compliment anyone's given you?

Imagine you're writing an op-ed about our world to be published in 2100.
What would you tell those generations by way of wisdom and warnings?

What's the biggest physical risk
you've ever taken?

What's the most insincere you've
ever been?

Write about the worst time you got
fired from your job.

What's your guiltiest pleasure?

You have an opportunity to have dinner with someone you love who is no longer alive. Who is it, and what kind of conversation did you have?

Do you believe in love at first sight? Defend your position.

What's the most spiteful thing you've done?

Who in your life do you consider your most trusted advisers
(your cabinet, so to speak)? In what ways, and why?

Write the obituary for your first car.

What is your favorite place in the world? Describe traveling
there with your worst enemy.

You're standing in your mother's (or father's, or aunt's) closet. Tell us what's on the floor, the hangers, the shelves. What does it smell like? Where is this place, and how old are you? Zero in on one object and write about it. How did it catch your attention?

Write a sincere and serious personals ad. Then rewrite it with humor.
Now rewrite it so that absolutely no one would reply.

What do you love most about your mother?

What was on your bedroom wall when you were a teenager?

If you had a voodoo doll, who would it be of?

Your great-great-grandchild is hunting through ancient Internet archives for records of you. She finds an e-mail you wrote; it shows her something about you that makes her stop and think about what living life in 2015 must have been like, and how people back then really had feelings and problems similar to those of people in 2200. Write that e-mail now.